In the Matter of the Petition of George N. Thornton, for a Writ of Mandamus

Edward C. Henderson

In the Matter of the Petition of George N. Thornton, for a Writ of Mandamus

Supreme Court of the United States - October Term, 1899 - Ex parte - Matter of Thornton - Answer of Continental Trust Company of the City of New York, Respondent
Edward C. Henderson, Willard Parker Butler
NYB01820
Court Record
New York City Bar
c.1900

The Making of Modern Law collection of legal archives constitutes a genuine revolution in historical legal research because it opens up a wealth of rare and previously inaccessible sources in legal, constitutional, administrative, political, cultural, intellectual, and social history. This unique collection consists of three extensive archives that provide insight into more than 300 years of American and British history. These collections include:

Legal Treatises, 1800-1926: over 20,000 legal treatises provide a comprehensive collection in legal history, business and economics, politics and government.

Trials, 1600-1926: nearly 10,000 titles reveal the drama of famous, infamous, and obscure courtroom cases in America and the British Empire across three centuries.

Primary Sources, 1620-1926: includes reports, statutes and regulations in American history, including early state codes, municipal ordinances, constitutional conventions and compilations, and law dictionaries.

These archives provide a unique research tool for tracking the development of our modern legal system and how it has affected our culture, government, business – nearly every aspect of our everyday life. For the first time, these high-quality digital scans of original works are available via print-on-demand, making them readily accessible to libraries, students, independent scholars, and readers of all ages.

The BiblioLife Network

This project was made possible in part by the BiblioLife Network (BLN), a project aimed at addressing some of the huge challenges facing book preservationists around the world. The BLN includes libraries, library networks, archives, subject matter experts, online communities and library service providers. We believe every book ever published should be available as a high-quality print reproduction; printed on-demand anywhere in the world. This insures the ongoing accessibility of the content and helps generate sustainable revenue for the libraries and organizations that work to preserve these important materials.

The following book is in the "public domain" and represents an authentic reproduction of the text as printed by the original publisher. While we have attempted to accurately maintain the integrity of the original work, there are sometimes problems with the original work or the micro-film from which the books were digitized. This can result in minor errors in reproduction. Possible imperfections include missing and blurred pages, poor pictures, markings and other reproduction issues beyond our control. Because this work is culturally important, we have made it available as part of our commitment to protecting, preserving, and promoting the world's literature.

GUIDE TO FOLD-OUTS MAPS and OVERSIZED IMAGES

The book you are reading was digitized from microfilm captured over the past thirty to forty years. Years after the creation of the original microfilm, the book was converted to digital files and made available in an online database.

In an online database, page images do not need to conform to the size restrictions found in a printed book. When converting these images back into a printed bound book, the page sizes are standardized in ways that maintain the detail of the original. For large images, such as fold-out maps, the original page image is split into two or more pages

Guidelines used to determine how to split the page image follows:

• Some images are split vertically; large images require vertical and horizontal splits.
• For horizontal splits, the content is split left to right.
• For vertical splits, the content is split from top to bottom.
• For both vertical and horizontal splits, the image is processed from top left to bottom right.

IN THE

Supreme Court of the United States

IN THE MATTER OF THE PETITION

OF

GEORGE N THORNTON,

FOR A

WRIT OF MANDAMUS

Answer of Continental Trust Company of the City of New York, Respondent.

EDWARD C. HENDERSON,
WILLARD PARKER BUTLER,
*Solicitors and of Counsel for
the Continental Trust Co.*

In the Supreme Court of the United States,

IN THE MATTER

OF

The petition of GEORGE N THORNTON
for a writ of mandamus

The answer of the Continental Trust Company of
the City of New York, to the application of George N
Thornton for leave to file a petition for a writ of
mandamus directed to the Circuit Court of the United
States for the Northern District of Ohio and the several Judges thereof, respectfully shows as follows

FIRST   Subsequent to the entry by the Circuit
Court of the United States for the Northern District
of Ohio, Western Division, in the cause pending
therein between Continental Trust Company of the
City of New York and John M. Butler, complainants,
v Toledo, St Louis and Kansas City Railroad Company et al, respondents, No 1205 in Equity, of the
decree of April 1, 1898 foreclosing the first mortgage
of said respondent Railroad Company, set out in said
petition and the entry of the decretal order of May
16th, 1898, modifying said decree as set out in said
petition, appeals were prosecuted from said decree and
said decretal orders, to the United States Circuit
Court of Appeals for the Sixth Circuit, by the Toledo,
St Louis and Kansas City Railroad Company, Ferdi-

nand E Canda, Jules S Bache, the Rhode Island
Locomotive Works, the Rhode Island National
Bank and S H Kneeland, and a separate
appeal was also prosecuted therefrom by
Charles Hamlin and others, holders of preferred stock in said Railroad Company, who had
filed a cross bill in said action A further appeal was
also prosecuted therefrom to the same court by one
Dana A Rose, an alleged holder of said preferred
stock, who had sought to file an intervening petition
which had been stricken from the files as filed without
leave Said appeals were duly argued in said Circuit
Court of Appeals in December, 1898, and in July, 1899,
said Circuit Court of Appeals, on the appeal of said
Hamlin, modified said decree of April 1, 1898, so far as
the same had been modified by the decretal order of
May 16th, 1898, affirmed said decree on the appeal of
said other appellants, and dismissed said appeal of said
Rose

Thereafter applications were made to said Circuit
Court of Appeals for a rehearing of said appeal by said
Railroad Company and the other appellants joining
therein and of said appeal of said Rose Said applications were thereafter in October, 1899, in all respects
denied by said Circuit Court of Appeals

The applicants, the Toledo, St Louis and Kansas
City Railroad Company, and others joining therein
made party to said appeal, the petitioner, Thornton, to
whom among others then notice and petition of appeal
were directed, to whom the citation on appeal was
directed, and on whom said citation was served

On said appeal there was argued among other questions, the jurisdiction of said Circuit Court to entertain
said bill of foreclosure of the first mortgage of said
respondent Railroad Company, and the status of persons filing claims under the creditors bill of said Stout
and Purdy, with regard to said foreclosure bill, and
the proceedings thereunder, by reason of the consoli-
dation of said creditors bill and said foreclosure bill

Said Circuit Court of Appeals held, affirming said Circuit Court, that said Circuit Court had jurisdiction of said foreclosure bill as an original dependent bill, that persons filing claims under said creditors bill did not become parties to the foreclosure bill, and that a decree in said foreclosure bill might properly be entered and had properly been entered, without a decree on said creditors appeal

For said decision of said Circuit Court of Appeals, reference is made to the opinions of said Court reported in 95 Fed Rep 497 and on said application for a rehearing in 96 Fed Rep , 784

Thereafter the mandates of said Circuit Court of Appeals were sent to the Circuit Court of the United States for the Northern District of Ohio, Western Division, and such proceedings were had, that on or about November 13th 1899, decrees in accordance with said mandates were entered in said Court Said decrees on said mandates are the decrees of November 13, 1899, referred to in the application of said Thornton

Thereafter and in the month of January, 1900, said Toledo, St Louis and Kansas City Railroad Company, The Rhode Island National Bank, The Rhode Island Locomotive Works, The Building and Contracting Co of Kentucky, Jules S Bache, Ferdinand E Canda, and Sylvester H Kneeland, as Petitioners, filed their petition in this court for a writ of *certiorari* to review said determination of said Circuit Court of Appeals, affirming on their said appeal to said Circuit Court of Appeals, said decree of foreclosure of April 1, 1898, and said Dana A Rose similarly filed a petition for a *certiorari* to review the determination of said Circuit Court of Appeals dismissing his said appeal to said Circuit Court of Appeals Said petitions were docketed in this court, as No 500 and 501 October Term, 1899 and were submitted on January 22, 1900 Said petitions were denied by this court on January 29, 1900 By each of said petitions it was sought to review the determination of said Circuit Court of

Appeals sustaining the jurisdiction of said Circuit Court to entertain said foreclosure bill as an original dependent bill, and denying to persons filing claims under the creditors bill, the status of parties to the foreclosure bill

For the contents of said petition for writs of *certiorari* and for the questions submitted thereby to this court, reference is made to said petitions and the printed record of proceedings in the Circuit Court of Appeals and the briefs submitted thereon, of record in this court

Before the submission to this court, of said applications for *certiorari*, said Thornton on January 11, 1900 presented to said Circuit Court his petition to expunge said decree of April 1, 1898, said decretal order of May 16, 1898, and said decrees of November 13, 1899 entered on said mandates of said Circuit Court of Appeals

Said petition was stricken from the files in accordance with an opinion of the Hon A J RICKS, District Judge in which the Hon WILLIAM H TAFT, Circuit Judge, concurred A copy of said opinion is filed herewith marked A

The grounds for said disposition of said petition were ,—

(a) that said petitioner was not a party to the foreclosure bill and had no standing to make such application ,

(b) that said petitioner had been made a party to said appeal to the Circuit Court from said decree of April 1, 1898 and said decretal order of May 16, 1898,

(c) that any application of such character after the appeal to the Circuit Court of Appeals and the determination of said Court, was made too late ,

(d) that the hearing having been had and decrees signed at Cincinnati, by the consent and with the acquiescence of all parties entitled to be heard thereon, were regular under the authority of *Doggett vs Emerson, 1 Wood & M 1, 7 Fed Cases, 819 ,*

(e) that the application was made in bad faith

Thereupon said Circuit Court at said Toledo, in the Northern District of Ohio, Western Division, in open court in term, by its decree made on that day, a copy of which is submitted herewith, marked B, re-entered and confirmed its said decrees of November 13, 1899 on said mandates of said Circuit Court of Appeals

THIRD Thereafter said petitioner attempted to file a notice of a motion to dismiss said foreclosure bill for lack of jurisdiction and assigned as grounds therefor, the same grounds which had been previously argued in said Circuit Court and determined adversely to the contention of said petitioner by said Circuit Court and by said Circuit Court of Appeals and by this Court, but said motion was denied by the Circuit Court, to which petitioner excepted Thereupon petitioner filed a petition praying an appeal to this Court, which petition was stricken from the files of said Circuit Court

FOURTH Thereafter petitioner, pursuant to leave given by the Court presented a so-called certificate of evidence or bill of exceptions, but the Circuit Court declined to sign the same or permit the same to be filed as appears from an opinion of the Hon A J Ricks, District Judge, in which the Hon W H Taft Circuit Judge, concurred A copy of said opinion is submitted herewith marked ' C " The aforesaid petitions, motions and bills of exceptions, were again presented to the Circuit Court substantially in the same form on February 12, 1900, and all of the papers were stricken from the files and the prayers of the petitions denied

FIFTH The claim of said petitioner under said creditors bill was filed Nov 29, 1897, prior to the date of the entry of the decree of foreclosure in the foreclosure suit on April 11, 1898

Wherefore respondent prays that said application for leave to file said petition for mandamus may be denied

Dated New York, February 23, 1900

      CONTINENTAL TRUST CO OF THE CITY OF NEW YORK

                by

                  WILLARD V KING

                          Secretary

E C HENDERSON

WILLARD PARKER BUTLER

      Solicitors and of Counsel for the Continental Trust Co of the City of New York, Respondent, 59 Wall Street, N Y City

———

UNITED STATES OF AMERICA, ⎫
Southern District of New York, ⎬ ss
CITY AND COUNTY OF NEW YORK ⎭

      WILLARD V KING being duly sworn, says

      That he is the Secretary of the Continental Trust Company of the City of New York, by whom the foregoing answer is filed , that he has read the foregoing answer and knows the contents thereof, and that the same is true of his own knowledge except as to the matters therein stated to be alleged upon information and belief and as to those matters he believes it to be true

      That the reason why this verification is made by depondent and not by said Trust Company is that the Trust Company is a corporation and deponent is an officer thereof

      The sources of my information and the grounds of my belief as to all matters not stated of my own knowledge are derived from the records in the aforesaid case, the records of said Trust Company and the correspondence of the Trust Company in deponent's possession

Sworn to before me this 24th ⎫ *Willard V. King*
  day of February, 1900   ⎬
                JOHN FRENCH
  (L S)   Notary Public
                    County of New York

Schedule " A."

IN THE
CIRCUIT COURT OF THE UNITED STATES

For the Northern District of Ohio,

Western Division

The Continental Trust Company
of New York, &c

vs

The Toledo, St Louis and Kansas
City Railroad Company, et al

PETITION TO EXPUNGE DECREES OF GEORGE N THORNTON AND FRANKLIN J SAWYER

Before Taft, Circuit Judge and Ricks, District Judge

This is a petition filed by George N Thornton and Franklin J Sawyer to expunge from the record of this court decrees for sale entered in the above-entitled cause on April 1 1898, the modification of that decree entered May 16, 1898, another decree of sale on the creditors' bill of Stout & Purdy, entered May 16, 1898, and two decrees of November 13, 1899, in execution of the mandate of the Circuit Court of Appeals affirming the three first-mentioned decrees, on the ground that William H Taft, Circuit Judge, whom the record shows to have been present at Toledo when said decrees were entered, was not present and did not hold court as therein recited, but was in Cincinnati and directed the decrees to be entered by letter written from Cincinnati to the clerk at Toledo

The above-entitled litigation has been pending in the Circuit Court of this district and in the Court of Appeals of this circuit for now seven years A full account of the litigation may be had by reference to the opinions of this court, to be found under the above title, 82 Fed Rep , 642 , 86 Fed Rep , 929, and to the opinion of Judge LURTON, speaking for the Court of Appeals, reported under the title of The Toledo, St Louis & Kansas City Railroad Company vs Continental Trust Company, in the 95th Federal Reporter, 497

Shortly stated, the litigation was begun by a general creditors' bill of Stout & Purdy, judgment creditors of the Toledo, St Louis & Kansas City Railroad Company, against the railroad company Under this bill a receiver was appointed, and thereafter a dependent bill was filed by The Continental Trust Company, in this court, to foreclose a first mortgage upon the defendant company's property securing $9,000,000 of its bonds The cause was delayed because of the controversy raised by preferred stockholders claiming the right to appear by answer and by cross-bill in their own interest as distinguished from that of the common stockholders who controlled the defendant company and its answer The controversy was taken to the court of appeals and there decided under the name of Hamlin vs Continental Trust Co , 47 U S A , 422 , 78 Fed Rep , 664 When the mandate in the Hamlin case came down, the district judge for this district was absent from the district on account of his health Therefore all the then parties to the record applied to Judge TAFT to hear the cause and to pass upon certain preliminary motions necessary to shape the cause for hearing Notice was duly given to all parties of a hearing at Cincinnati before Judge Taft, all the parties to the record appeared, either in person or by counsel, and the hearing was had in Cincinnati The case was fully argued in behalf of every interest, and thereafter the court filed an op-

9

ion in which the orders to be made were fully indicated This is the opinion reported in 82 Fed Rep, 642

Upon due notice to all parties a further hearing was had at Cincinnati as to the form of the orders to be made, and a motion to modify the orders was made by those asserting the invalidity of the mortgage and the bonds issued thereunder The orders were accordingly modified, and, upon being signed, were sent from Cincinnati to Toledo One of these orders directed the master therefore appointed to advertise for claims of creditors under the prayer of the general creditors' bill, and the master was directed to report the claims made, and it was permitted that each creditor be allowed to object to the claims of other creditors in accordance with the practice in equity Another order allowed judgment creditors, as parties to the creditors bill, to file intervening petitions against the trustee under the mortgage, attacking the validity of the bonds secured thereby Issues were made on these intervening petitions by answers and replications, and an immense mass of testimony was taken on them

When all the proof had been taken, upon due notice to every party to the record, a final hearing was had at Cincinnati, and every party to the record was present in person or by counsel at the hearing, and full argument was made on behalf of every interest, and briefs were subsequently submitted An elaborate opinion reported in 86 Fed Rep, 929, was mailed from Cincinnati to Toledo by Judge Taft, and it was filed there After the opinion had been on file for some weeks, notice was duly served by counsel for the complainant trust company upon all the parties to the record, both in the foreclosure suit and in the creditors' bill, that a motion would be made before Judge Taft, at Cincinnati, for a settlement and entry of the decree, all the parties appeared either in person or by counsel, and the decree was settled at Cincinnati and was sent from there by the judge to Toledo, to be entered, and it was entered, as all the parties understood it would be, as if the hearing had been had at Toledo and the judge had been present there Subsequently a modification of the decree was made affecting only the issue between the common stockholders and the preferred stockholders, and the modification was made after due notice to Kneeland, who had filed an answer and cross-bill on behalf of the common stockholders

Upon the same day a decree was entered upon the creditors' bill ordering the sale under the foreclosure to stand as the sale under the creditors' bill, and remitting the question of priority as between the claims filed under the creditors' bill until after the sale of the property This was entered after due notice to all the parties of record in the creditors' bill

Thereafter, on May 3, 1898, as appears by the records of this court, a petition for the allowance of an appeal was filed by the Building and Contracting Company of Kentucky and the Rhode Island Locomotive Works, by Potter & Emery, William B Sanders and J D Springer, their solicitors , the Rhode Island National Bank and the Signal Oil Works, Limited, by William B Sanders and J D Springer, their solicitors , Ferdinand E Canda, by Smith & Baker, William B Sanders, and J D Springer, his solicitors Accompanying this petition was filed an assignment of errors, seventy-one in number Subsequent to this the decree, as already stated, was modified on May 16, 1898, and the decree of the creditors' bill was entered

Thereafter the petition for the allowance of the appeal came on to be heard, and it was found by the court that all the parties to the record had been notified of the application for the appeal, and that notice of the application had also been served on all the persons who had filed their claims before the master as creditors under the creditors' bill among whom were George N Thornton and Frank J Sawyer, the petitioners at the bar

At the hearing of this petition seventeen additional assignments of error were filed, and others of the peties to the record, together with one creditor who had filed his claim under the creditors' bill, became parties to the appeal. The appeal was allowed and special orders made for the citation of the parties

Thereafter all the parties to the record were served with citation, as well as all the persons filing their claims before the master. Among the persons thus cited upon appeal who had filed their claims before the master were George N Thornton and Franklin J Sawyer, the petitioners here. Thornton and Sawyer had filed objections to the claims of the trust company before the master. No objection was made of record or orally, or in any way at any time, to the settling and entry of the decrees at Cincinnati before Judge TAFT, in his chambers at that place, and the decrees signed by him were therefore entered at Toledo as if he were present at that place.

Thereafter the eighty-eight assignment of error were filed on appeal, and no mention was made in any way of this alleged irregularity as an objection to the validity of the decrees. The appeal was taken, four thousand printed pages of the record were transcribed and carried into the court of appeals, and there printed. The cause was heard at length in the court of appeals. No objection of the kind here made was made, orally or of record, in that court to the decrees, and judgment was rendered in the court of appeals, affirming in every material respect, except a provision as to the preferred stockholders, the decrees entered in the court below, and the mandate of the circuit court of appeals was sent down, directing the execution of the decrees in accordance with its opinion and the modification of it indicated therein.

After the mandate reached the circuit court, counsel for the complainant trust company issued a notice to all the parties of record in the circuit court of their intention to apply to Judge TAFT at Cincinnati for a settlement and entry of the decree and order upon the mandate of the circuit court of appeals. All of the parties appeared or were represented by counsel, and the decree was there settled   Among the counsel present was Mr J D Springer, who appears of record in the case as counsel and solicitor for Franklin J Sawyer, one of the petitioners, and a claimant and objector before the master, though he does not sign this petition   Mr Springer does, however, make an affidavit, which is filed in support of the petition, in which he says that before the appeal in the cause was taken, he was in Toledo and examined the decrees, and found that the record recited the fact of Judge Taft's presence in Toledo, when he knew that he was in Cincinnati, and that he learned that this was the customary mode of entering decrees in such cases   Mr Springer was leading counsel for many creditors, and most active in opposition to the foreclosure of the mortgage and collection of the bonds

The last decree was entered November 13, 1899, and on the 18th day of December these petitions are filed, and proof is offered to sustain the averments of them by the affidavits of S H Kneeland, J D Springer, John Ford, counsel for Kneeland, and the clerk of the court   Each of the petitions avers

> "That your petitioner was not notified of, and in nowise participated in, any of the said acts or proceedings before the said the Hon William H Taft aforesaid, and in nowise consented to any action being taken therein by the said the Hon William H Taft, and has never in anywise consented to the determination of his rights by or before the said the Hon. William H Taft, nor has he in anywise waived or relinquished his right to the determination of his rights in the premises by this court"

BY THE COURT

These petitions will be stricken from the files for the reason that they were filed without leave of court and by persons who are not parties to the cause in this court

The consolidated case was made up of two causes, one a foreclosure suit and the other a creditors' bill The petitioners were not parties to the foreclosure suit They were not made parties by the bill of complaint, and they did not attempt to and were not allowed to intervene by petition They were mere general creditors who had no right to be heard on the issue of foreclosure between the trustee of the mortgage and the defendant railroad company They had attained no lien on the property, by judgment or otherwise, and were not entitled to resist the prayer of foreclosure So much for the foreclosure decree

As to the decree on the creditors' bill, they were not parties to the record They filed no intervening petition, and all they did was to appear before the master and file their claims and make objection to other claims They were but quasi-parties and have no right to be heard in this cause, except after leave obtained of the court

This would dispose of the petitions, but we prefer also to consider them on their merits It is unnecessary for us to consider the question whether it is within the power of a circuit judge to direct the entry of a decree of sale in one district of his circuit when he is sitting in another without the consent or acquiescence of the parties It is clear that, by consent of the parties, a cause in equity may be finally heard and decided by a circuit judge within his circuit, but outside of the district in which the cause is pending In Doggett vs Emerson et al, 1 Woodb & M 1, 7 Fed Cases, 819, Mr Justice WOODBURY had occasion to consider the validity of a final hearing by Mr Justice STORY of a suit in equity pending in the district of Maine, which was heard, by agreement of parties, before the circuit judge, in vacation, at Boston, and it was said in that case that no one of the parties consenting to such hearing could impeach the validity of the hearing and decree on account of the time or the place at which the hearing was had, and the decree was directed to be made Speaking of the opinion rendered upon such a hearing, the court said

> "It shows what is the decree of the court as much as an opinion, read by one of the judges in the court-room, containing the views of the court, shows the opinion of the court If both are completed and announced to the parties at the time and place agreed by them, they are finished, except the mere entry of them on the docket and record The subsequent steps are rather steps to enforce or carry them into effect, than parts of the decree and opinion themselves "

No such authority was necessary, however, in courts of the United States to sustain the view that where parties consent to the final hearing of the cause before a circuit judge whose jurisdiction is throughout the entire circuit, such consent authorizes the entry of the decree in the court where the cause is pending and upon its records, as if the cause had been heard in open court at that place No other construction can be put upon the consent of the parties to have the final hearing at some other place than that fixed by law It has been the uniform practice in this circuit in equity causes for parties to consent to the final hearing of them outside of the district in which they are pending, at some convenient point in the circuit before the circuit judge, and after consideration, and upon decision, to enter the decree by direction of the judge at the place of holding court in the district, as if the judge had been present at the time of hearing the cause and entering the decree Such practice has been of the greatest convenience to parties and to the judge It has facilitated the business of the circuit and made it possible for the circuit judges, whose time has been chiefly taken in appell work, to assist their brethren, the district judges, in their work in the various districts, in the disposition of causes which in their nature might be as easily heard at one point as another in the circuit. Patent suits in equity and suits for the foreclosure of railroads usually involve the attendance of counsel, most of whom do not reside at the place of holding court, and it is as convenient for such counsel after the record is made up to attend the judge at one point in the circuit as at another, and not to wait until such time as he may be able to be present in the district where the cause is pending. If it were to be held that decrees entered in accordance with such practice were null and void and might be impeached by affidavits or other evidence tending to show that the judge whose presence was recited in the record was in some other part of the circuit upon the day on which the decree in the cause was entered, it is not too much to say that there are many decrees upon which vast interests are dependent for title and security, and of many years' standing, which will still be subject to impeachment as void.

The proof upon this motion shows conclusively, and it is within the personal knowledge of one member of this court who entered the decrees, that every party to the record was represented at the many hearings which were held, both interlocutory and final, and at the settlement of the several decrees which were made, and that it was clearly understood by all the parties that the final decree was to be entered at Toledo exactly as if the presiding judge had been present in person at that place. It follows, therefore, that all the parties to the record are bound by the recital of the record, and are estopped to deny it.

But how is the case of the petitioners? They assert that they were parties to the record, and received no notice of the hearings or of the settlement of the decrees at Cincinnati. In the first place, Sawyer, one of the petitioners, has as his counsel and solicitor Mr. J. D. Springer, who was present in the court-room and in

the judge s chambeis at Cincinnati on every occasion
when any hearing was had, when any oidei was made
when any decree was settled In the second place,
both Sawyer and Thornton were, out of abundant caution, biought in by citation to the appellate pioceed-
ings, and were given an opportunity to join in the appeal They weie thus advised of the decrees which
had been entered, and had full oppoitunity to appeal
theiefiom and to be heard upon such appeal, and one
person sim/laily situated with them, Chailes Millei,
who was only a geneial cieditoi, having filed his claim
before the mastei, was allowed to appeal from the decrees theietofoie enteied Notwithstanding this, the
petitioners made no objection in the court of appeals
that the decrees entered had not been regulaily enteied according to law As these petitioners weie
given an opportunity to join in that appeal and declined to do so, the order and mandate of the appellate court is as binding upon them as it is upon any
of the persons who were regularly parties to the
record

Moieovei, this court has no powei to modify or
supersede in the slightest degree the decieees which
bear the imprimatur of the court of appeals (In ie
Potts, 166 U S, 263, Sandtord Fork & Tool Co, peti-
tionei 160 U S, 247) It is the duty of this couit
simply to execute the mandate of that court

It cannot annul its decrce after the expiration of the
term at which it was enteied (Sibbald vs U S, 12
Peteis, 488)

The Supieme Court of the United States has said
that—

"On a mandate from this court affiiming
a decree the circuit court can only iecoid
our order, and proceed with the execution
of its own decree as affirmed It has no
powei to rescind or modify what we have
established * * * After the appeal had been

taken, the power of the court below under its own decree was gone All it could do after that was to obey our mandate when it was sent down We affirmed its decree and ordered its execution '

In accordance with that duty, the decree of November 13, 1899, was entered It was settled at Cincinnati after due notice to all the parties to the record, and without objection by any of them, in accordance with the course which had been taken with respect to every hearing in the case after the cause had first been submitted to Judge Taft So far as the foreclosure decree is concerned, the petitioners are not parties to it in any way, and they have no standing to impeach it for any reason So far as the creditors' bill is concerned and the decree of the court executing the mandate of the court of appeals upon that, their position is no better They were not parties to the record and, so far as the regularity of the decree is concerned, they are bound by the consent of the complainant in the creditors' bill, and the other parties thereto who, for such purpose are representative of the whole class of creditors

It would be the grossest injustice to the parties to this cause in whose favor those decrees have been pronounced and who have, in the well-founded belief, induced thereto by the consent and conduct of their real opponents, that hearings had and decrees settled at Cincinnati were to be recorded at Toledo as if held or passed at the latter place, expended much time, money, and labor to bring this protracted and burdensome litigation to an end, now to hold that the decrees are as waste paper

For the reasons given, the petitions are held to have no merit in them, and, having been filed without leave, they are stricken from the files

This action of the court meets the present emergency, and we should be content to leave the matter as it is, were it not that these petitions, considered in the light of all the circumstances, justify the suspicion that some of the defeated litigants in this cause are willing to evade the estoppel against obstructive proceedings which considerations of propriety and good faith to their adversaries and the court would necessarily create by the instigation of others with comparatively little interest in the litigation to a course of obstruction in which it is hoped they may not be met by the estoppel, and which, if successful, will inure to the benefit of all the defeated litigants Counsel may be easily changed, and new counsel employed who can deny any consent to proceedings of the court which were induced by the consent and acquiescence of the retiring counsel

We propose, therefore, to remove every shadow of a ground, however slight and unfounded, which the desperation of defeated litigants may seize upon or the astuteness of compliant counsel may suggest for future attack upon the regularity of these decrees Therefore, out of abundant caution, we shall re-enter and confirm the decrees of November 13, 1899, as of this day Under that decree the advertisement for the sale has begun and the date fixed as of the fourteenth day of February next Some expense has been incurred thereby Nevertheless, an order will be entered directing the masters to cease the advertisement begun The decree of November 13, 1899, will be modified so as to extend the time within which the sale may take place to the second of April next, and the special masters are authorized and directed to fix a day for the sale, within the time limited, so that due advertisement under the decree may be had before the sale, and to begin a new advertisement accordingly Proper entries have been prepared by the court, and will be entered by the clerk forthwith

The full brief of counsel for the petitioners and all the evidence offered in support of their motions have been submitted to Judge TAFT, and he joins in

in this opinion and fully concurs therein, and also with
the orders and decrees this day entered

(Signed)   AUGUSTUS J RICKS,
U S District Judge, Sitting in Circuit Court

[ENDORSED] United States circuit court, northern
district of Ohio, western division The Continental
Trust Co of New York, vs The Toledo, St Louis &
Kansas City Railroad Company *et al* Copy of opinion of the court

---

Schedule " B."

UNITED STATES CIRCUIT COURT,

NORTHERN DISTRICT OF OHIO, WESTERN DIVISION

CONTINENTAL TRUST COMPANY &c

v

TOLEDO ST LOUIS & KANSAS CITY
R R Co

Came again the parties herein and it appearing to
the Court by the petitions of Sawyer and Thornton
which by order of the court have been stricken from
the files as appears by the entry of the court this day
made, that some question has been made as to the
regularity and validity of the decrees entered on the
13th day of November 1899 in this cause it is ordered
out of abundant caution that said decrees which are
  follows to wit

This day came again the parties and the mandate
' the United States Circuit Court of Appeals for the
' ixth Circuit on the appeal of the Toledo, St Louis

and Kansas City Railroad Company, Building and
Contracting Company of Kentucky, Rhode Island
Locomotive Works, The Rhode Island National Bank,
the Signal Oil Works, Limited, Ferdinand E Canda
Jules S Bache and S H Kneeland, having been filed
in this court on the 11th day of October, 1899, it is in
accordance with said mandate ordered, adjudged and
decreed, that the decree of this court entered in this
cause on April 1st, 1898, as modified by the orders of
this court entered in this cause on the 16th day of
May, 1898, be and the same hereby is in all things
affirmed, and that the complainant, Continental Trust
Company, of the City of New York, recover of said
appellants St Louis and Kansas City Railroad Company, Building and Contracting Company of Kentucky,
Rhode Island Locomotive Works, the Rhode Island
National Bank, Signal Oil Works, Ltd Ferdinand E
Canda, Jules S Bache and S H Kneeland

The costs of said complaint, to be taxed and entered
in this decree and that said complainant have execution therefor

This day come again the parties and the mandate
of the United States Circuit Court of Appeals for the
sixth Circuit on the appeal of the cross-complainants
Charles Hamlin, Hannibal E Hamlin, Frank Hamlin
and Ellen V Hamlin from the decree of this Court entered in this cause on April 1, 1898, having been filed
in this Court on the 11th day of October, 1899,

It is, in accordance with said mandate,

Ordered, adjudged and decreed, that the decree of
this Court entered in this cause on April 1, 1898, be
and the same hereby is modified by striking from said
decree the modification thereof granted by this court
by its order entered on the 16th day of May, 1898, in
the words and figures following, to-wit —

Upon the issue arising between the cross-bill of said
Hamlins and others and the answer to said cross bill
of the defendants the Toledo, St Louis and Kansas
City Railroad Company and the answer of S H Knee-

land, for himself and other common stockholders, the court finds that said cross-complainants and others as holders of the preferred stock in the said Toledo, St Louis and Kansas City Railroad Company have, by virtue of the terms under which said stock was issued, a priority over said common stockholders, not only in the payment of dividends, but also in the distribution of the assets, remaining after the payment of all the debts of said company secured or otherwise, when the same may come on to be distributed and therefore, that if said preferred stockholders or any of them chose to do so they may deposit in partial fulfillment of any bid which they may make at the sale ordered herein shares of the preferred stock of said railroad Company, provided, however, that such stock shall not be received for this purpose until the holders thereof shall have paid into the registry of the Court a sum upon their bid in cash, sufficient to satisfy all the costs and expenses of this suit and sale, all the receivers' debts, all the mortgage debts, and all the debts, claims for which have been filed either in this foreclosure proceeding, or under the creditors' bill consolidated herewith, with interest thereon to the day of distribution, as said debts have been or shall be hereafter adjudicated either under the foreclosure bill or the creditors' bill herein—and provided further that said preferred stock thus deposited shall be received to pay only that part of the surplus of the bid after payment of the debts of the railroad company which its owners would be entitled to receive on their shares of stock in the distribution of the surplus among the holders of the entire issue of said preferred stock, and the remainder of said surplus, to be paid in cash, shall be held for ratable distribution to the owners of the shares of preferred stock not joining in the bid, and provided further that as a condition of the privilege of using the preferred stock to complete their bid as above permitted, such preferred stockholders shall, if they become the purchasers of the said mortgaged railroad ordered sold, hold said road thus purchased subject to a lien equal in amount to the entire surplus remaining out of the purchase price bid after the payment of all the costs, expenses receivers' debts and debts of the company, mortgage or otherwise filed and adjudicated herein, to secure the payment of any debts of said Toledo, St Louis and Kansas City Railroad Company, which have not been presented under this bill or the creditor's bill herein as the holders of said claims may present them and establish their validity, and the Court reserves the right to retake the mortgaged property again into its possession to enforce the payment of said debts as they are presented until the said surplus shall have been exhausted

And it is further ordered, adjudged and decreed that in lieu thereof there be added to the foot of said decree of April 1, 1898, the following provision

Upon application made by and on behalf of the cross-complainant Hannibal E Hamlin and others for a modification of the decree of foreclosure entered April 1, 1898, the Court grants the application by adding at the foot of said decree the following

Upon the issue arising between the cross-bill of said Hamlins and others and the answer to said cross-bill of the defendant the Toledo, St Louis and Kansas City Railroad Company, and the answer of S H Kneeland, for himself and other common stockholders the Court finds that said cross-complainants and others as holders of the preferred stock in said Toledo, St Louis and Kansas City Railroad Company have, by virtue of the terms under which said stock was issued a priority over said common stockholders, not only in the payment of dividends, but also in the distribution of the assets remaining after the payment of all the debts of said company, secured or otherwise, when the same may come on to be distributed, and, therefore, that said preferred stockolders or any of them chose to do so they may deposit, in partial fulfillment of any b which they may make at the sale ordered herein, shares of the preferred stock of said railroad company Provided, however, that such stock shall not be received for this purpose until the holders thereof shall have paid into the registry of the Court a sum upon their bid in cash sufficient to satisfy all the costs and expenses of this suit and sale, all the Receiver's debts, all the mortgage debts and all the debts, claims for which have been filed either in this foreclosure proceeding or under the creditor's bill consolidated herewith, with interest thereon to the day of distribution, as said debts have been, or shall be hereafter adjudicated, either under the foreclosure bill or the creditors bill herein, and provided further, that said preferred stock thus deposited shall be received to pay only that part of the surplus of the bid after payment of debts of the railroad company which its owners would be entitled to receive on their shares of stock in the distribution of the surplus among the holders of the entire issue of said preferred stock, and the remainder of said surplus, to be paid in cash shall be held for ratable distribution to the owners of the shares of preferred stock not joining in the bid, and provided further, that as a condition of the privilege of using the preferred stock to complete their bid as above permitted, such preferred stockholders shall if they become the purchasers of the said mortgaged railroad ordered sold, hold said road thus purchased subject to a lien equal in amount to the entire surplus remaining out of the purchase price bid after the payment of all costs, expenses, receiver's debts, and debts of the company, mortgage or otherwise, filed and adjudicated herein, or which hereafter may be filed and adjudicated and which may be presented under the foreclosure bill or the creditor's bill herein, in accordance with the following direction

In the event of the purchase of the mortgaged property herein ordered to be sold, by the preferred stockholders, such purchasers shall forthwith give notice by publication, once a week for four consecutive weeks, in four newspapers published respectively in the cities of New York, Toledo, Indianapolis and Springfield, stating such purchase and the effect of this decree and calling upon all creditors of the mortgagor, Railroad Company not parties to the cause, to present their claims to the Court by filing the same duly verified, with the Clerk of this Court, within six months from the date of such first publication, which is hereby determined to be a reasonable time for that purpose

And the Court in the event of such purchase by the preferred stockholders of the respondent, The Toledo, St Louis and Kansas City Railroad Company, reserves the right to retake and resell the mortgaged property to enforce such lien for the payment of said debts due said creditors as they may be presented and established until the said surplus shall have been exhausted

And it being made to appear to the Court that since the entry of the decree of foreclosure herein, the Special Masters herein appointed to make sale of the mortgaged property, being Messrs Hiram D Peck and William A Van Buren, have resigned their said appointments, it is therefore ordered and decreed that Frank H Shaffer of Cincinnati, Ohio, and Merrill Moores of Indianapolis, Indiana, be and they are hereby appointed to fill the vacancies occasioned by the resignation of the said Peck and Van Buren, the said Shaffer and Moores to have and exercise all the powers vested by the final decree of foreclosure and all other orders and decrees of this Court in the said originally appointed Special Masters

And it further appearing to the satisfaction of the Court, that it will be to the best interests of all the parties interested in the said Railroad, equipment and franchises, that the same shall be sold by the Special Masters appointed for said purpose within a period of time to be fixed by the Court, it is further ordered adjudged and decreed that the said Merrill Moores and Frank H Shaffer shall sell the same in accordance with the fourth article of the said decree at a date to be fixed by them not later than the 15th day of February, 1900

It is further ordered and decreed that the costs of said appellants in said appeal when taxed to be paid by the Receiver in this cause

' This day come again the parties and the mandate " of the United States Circuit Court of Appeals for the " sixth Circuit, on the appeal heretofore taken from " the decree entered in this cause on the 1st day of " April, 1898, by Dana A Rose, having been filed in ' this court on the 11th day of October, 1899

" It is, in accordance with said mandate,

" Ordered adjudged and decreed that the decree of " this court entered in this cause on April 1, 1898, be " and the same hereby is affirmed and that the com- " plainant, Continental Trust Company of the City of " New York, recover of said appellant, Dana A Rose," " the costs of said complainant to be taxed, and that " complainant have execution therefor

' together with the modification this day made which ' is as follows

" This day came again the parties and for good cause " shown it is ordered that the decrees of this court ' heretofore entered on the 13th of November 1899 ' directing a compliance with the mandate of the court ' of Appeals filed herein and a sale of the railroad ' and property of the defendant company be modified " so that the time within which said sale shall take " place shall be extended to the 2nd day of April 1900 ' and the Masters appointed to conduct the sale are ' directed to discontinue the advertising already " begun in which the sale is fixed for the 14th day of ' February 1900 and they are directed after fixing the " day of sale more than six weeks from the date hereof " to begin a new advertisement in accordance with the " terms of the decree of April 1st, 1898, as modified and supplemented by the decrees of May 16th, 1898, ' and the decree of November 13th, 1899 " be reentered and confirmed as the decree of this court in compliance with the mandate of the Circuit Court of Appeals heretofore filed

————

THE UNITED STATES OF AMERICA,
    Northern District of Ohio,   } ss
      WESTERN DIVISION,

I, IRVIN BELFORD, Clerk of the Circuit Court of the United States within and for said District and Division do hereby certify that the foregoing contains a true and complete copy of the Order, re-entering and confirming the Decrees, heretofore entered, entered in the therein entitled cause on January 19, 1900

Witness my official signature and the seal of said Court at Toledo, in said District this 20th day of January, A D 1900, and the 124th year of the Independence of the United States of America

[SEAL]   IRVIN BELFORD,
                                   Clerk,
             By J W WILSON,
                       Deputy Clerk

Schedule " C."

IN THE CIRCUIT COURT OF THE UNITED STATES,

FOR THE NORTHERN DISTRICT OF OHIO, WESTERN DIVISION

THE CONTINENTAL TRUST CO , OF
NEW YORK, &c ,

v

THE TOLEDO, ST LOUIS & KANSAS
CITY RAILROAD COMPANY, ET AL

} 1205

MEMORANDUM

RICKS D J

Since the 19th instant, when the last proceedings in this case took place at Toledo, in pursuance of special notice of counsel, I have taken pains to examine the authorities as to the duty of the trial judge in the Circuit Court of the United States to sign a bill of exceptions in an Equity cause I find the authorities are overwhelming in favor of the proposition that no such thing as a bill of exceptions is known in the Equity practice in the Federal Courts

The earliest, and the leading case, which passes upon this question, is the case of *er parte* Story, reported in 37 U S 339   That was a case where, on a mandate from the Supreme Court of the United States, the trial Judge in the Circuit Court refused to sign a bill of exceptions presenting the fact as to the death of Edward Livingston, one of the parties to the suit, which act became a material point in the case   As stated in the report of the case, upon the presentation of the bill of exceptions, the Judge remarked "that he would ' sign no bill of exceptions unless he was convinced

' that he was bound to sign one   Upon being subse-
' quently importuned upon the subject, he stated, if he
" signed a bill of exceptions, he must give the reasons
" at length for his opinion   He has been again and again
' importuned, and unsuccessfully, upon the subject
' That on this day your petitioner's counsel presented
" to the Court the annexed answer, &c , and desired
" that it might be placed upon the file in the cause ,
" but the Court refused permission to file the same
" Thereupon, the annexed bill of exceptions was ten-
' dered to the Judge, which bill truly stated the facts ,
" but the Judge refused to sign the same, or make it a
' part of the record   The Court was then moved to
" direct the Clerk of the Court to state the facts upon
" the order book , but the Court refused to suffer any
" notice to be taken of this matter, as a part of the
' proceedings in the Court , stating at the same time,
" that he considered a mandamus to be the true rem-
" edy , and alleging no other reason for not signing the
" bill of exceptions, or suffering notice to be taken of
" the presentation of the answer on the record "

On a motion for a mandamus, the Supreme Court
said —

" We think there is no sufficient ground for this application   A bill of exceptions is altogether unknown
in chancery practice , nor is a court of chancery bound
to inscribe in an order book, upon the application of
one of the parties, an order which it may pass in a
case before it , and the facts which the defendant stated
in the supplemental answer and plea which he offered
furnished no ground of defence in the Circuit Court,
when acting under the mandate of this Court, and car-
rying its directions into execution In the case of Skillern's Executors v May's Executors, 6 Cranch, 267, this
Court said, that as it appeared that the merits of the
case had been finally decided in this Court, and that its
mandate required only the execution of its decree , the
Circuit Court was bound to carry that decree into execution, although the jurisdiction of the Court was not

alleged in the pleadings In the case now before the Court, the merits of the controversy were finally decided by this Court, and its mandate to the District Court required only the execution of its decree The case, therefore, comes within the principle of Skillern's Executors v May's Executors, and the facts stated by the defendant cannot, in this stage of the proceedings, form any defence against the execution of the mandate, and consequently, he was not deprived of any legal or equitable ground of defence, by the refusal of the Court to suffer him to file the supplemental answer and plea which he offered The motion for the rule to show cause is therefore refused

In the case of Johnson v Harmon, 94 U S, 371, the Supreme Court, on application for a bill of exceptions, say —

" A bill of exceptions cannot be taken on the trial of a feigned issue directed by a Court of Equity or, if taken, can only be used on a motion for a new trial made to said Court 2 Dan Ch Pr (3d Am ed) 1106, Armstrong v Armstrong, 3 Myl & K 52, *Ex parte* Story, 12 Pet 343 See the cases on new trials on feigned issues collected in 3 " Graham & Waterman on New Trials, 1553, &c The issue is directed to be tried for the purpose of informing the conscience of the Chancellor and aiding him to come to a proper conclusion If he thinks the trial has not been a fair one, or for any other reason desires a new trial, it is in his discretion to order it But he may proceed with the cause though dissatisfied with the verdict, and make a decree contrary thereto, if in his judgment the law and the evidence so requires A decree in equity, therefore, when appealed from, does not stand or fall according to the legality or illegality of the proceedings on the trial of a feigned issue in the cause, for the verdict may or may not have been the ground of the decree It is the duty of the Court of first instance to decide (as was done here) upon the whole case, pleadings, evidence and verdict, giving to

the latter so much effect as it is worth An appeal
from the decree must be decided in the same way,
namely, upon the whole case, and cannot be made to
turn on the correctness or incorrectness of the Judge's
rulings at the trial of the feigned issue "

In the case of Watt v Starke, 101 U S 248, it was
said by the Supreme Court that the verdict upon an
issue which a Court of Chancery directs to be tried at
law is merely advisory A motion for new trial can be
made only to that Court, and the party submitting it
must procure, for the use of the Chancellor, notes of
the proceedings at the trial, and the evidence there
given The evidence and proceedings become, then,
part of the record, and are subject to review by the
appellate Court, should an appeal from the decree be
taken "

This is from the opinion of Mr Justice BRADLEY
who had examined very exhaustively all the cases reported, in which the question of the right of the appellant to have the bill of exceptions signed by the
trial Judge is involved In all these cases, it will be
observed, the Supreme Court basis its action upon the
theory that, in an Equity case, all of the proceedings,
pleadings and evidence are in writing, and therefore
make up a complete record of all the proceedings in
the case The Court, therefore, has no need of a bill
of exceptions, or any other form of certificate, in
deciding the case In an action at law the
record is made up in a different way In such
a case, the pleadings, of course, are a matter of
record The verdict of the Jury, and the motion to
set aside the verdict and for a new trial, are also a part
of the record , but, there being no rule or practice re-
quiring the evidence to be reduced to writing, the
Appellate Court, in a law case, has nothing to show
what was the testimony in the case This is supplied
by a bill of exceptions, which, when properly prepared
shows all the proceedings in the Court, except the
pleadings and the steps heretofore stated The Court

therefore unanimously hold that a bill of exceptions has no place in the record in an equity case. If there is any oral testimony offered on the trial of an equity case, and, owing to special conditions and circumstances, the Chancellor should allow such oral evidence, it would be supplied by some sort of a certificate or bill of exceptions; but this can only be done, as I have already stated, in a special case, where the Chancellor, in the discretion vested in him, makes a special order concerning the mode of presenting to the Court of review the oral testimony so taken.

That this is the ruling of the Courts of the United States is beyond all question; but, if we turn to the third volume of the Encyclopædia of Pleading and Practice, page 381, we find that the practice is almost as uniform in the State Courts, in refusing a bill of exceptions in such a case as this, as I have already shown it to be in the Federal Courts.

Under the subject of "Bills of Exceptions," a very elaborate review is made of all the authorities, in both the Federal and State Courts, in the Encyclopædia above referred to. The proposition stated is as follows:

"In equity, as the evidence and all objections thereto and all the orders and decrees of the Court, are in writing, under the technical Chancery practice, and are parts of the record proper. A bill of exceptions is improper, and, where taken, will be disregarded on appeal."

I do not know what counsel for the petitioners, Sawyer and Thornton, undertake to incorporate in their bill of exceptions.

I do not know what there is, outside of the record already made, that will enable them to present any more clearly to the reviewing Court the irregularities and errors complained of. Everything that has been offered in evidence at the various hearings which we have attended under the several notices of counsel is already a matter of record in this case, and all that is needed is that such record should be fully and properly presented to such Court of review

What has taken place at either of these hearings, by way of Colloquy, in open Court, is not a matter of record, and the Court ought not to certify to the correctness of such proceedings Such proceedings are not required by statute or practice, and the Court, when called upon, should refuse to certify the same, on the ground that they are not a part of the record, and therefore need not be certified

The refusal of the Court to allow the written applications for an appeal to the Supreme Court from the order striking the petition of Sawyer from the files is a matter of record, and therefore need not be specially certified No question of jurisdiction is involved in their cases, and the refusal to •certify cannot be error

The refusal to allow the written prayer for an appeal, on the motion to dismiss the bill of foreclosure for want of jurisdiction, to the Supreme Court of the United States, is a part of the record of the case, and therefore the holding of the Court is not error The parties lost their right to appeal to the Supreme Court on the question of jurisdiction by their appeal to the Circuit Court of Appeals

ᵗA information can be obtained at www.ICGtesting.com
ⁱn the USA
·1410080414

`V00011B/711/P